ORIGINAL KEYS
for SINGERS

MEN of Christmas

VOCAL/PIANO

ISBN 978-1-4584-1019-1

HAL•LEONARD®
CORPORATION

7777 W. BLUEMOUND RD. P.O. BOX 13819 MILWAUKEE, WI 53213

Visit Hal Leonard Online at
www.halleonard.com

BLUE CHRISTMAS

Words and Music by BILLY HAYES
and JAY JOHNSON

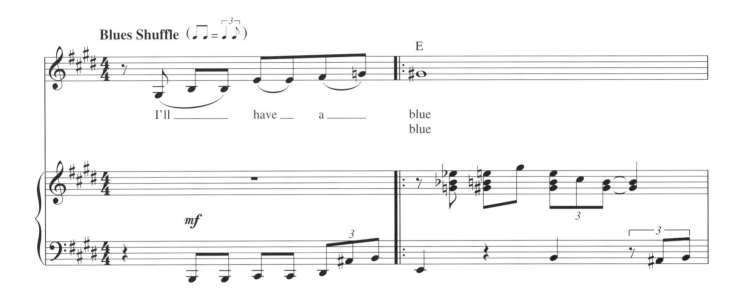

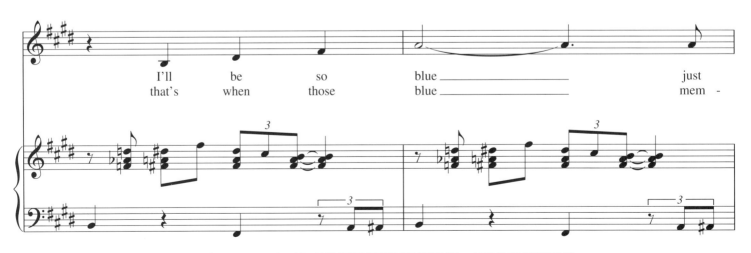

CAROLING, CAROLING

Words by WIHLA HUTSON
Music by ALFRED BURT

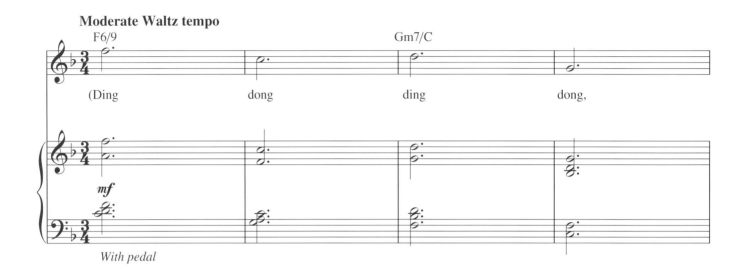

(Ding dong ding dong,

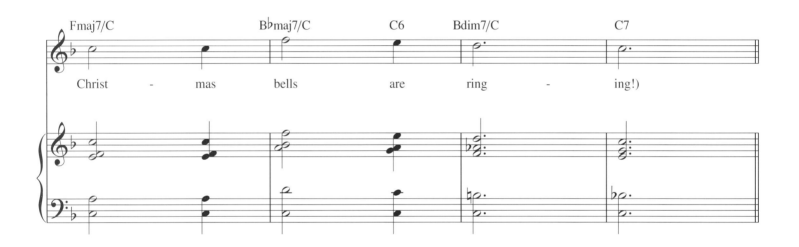

Christ - mas bells are ring - ing!)

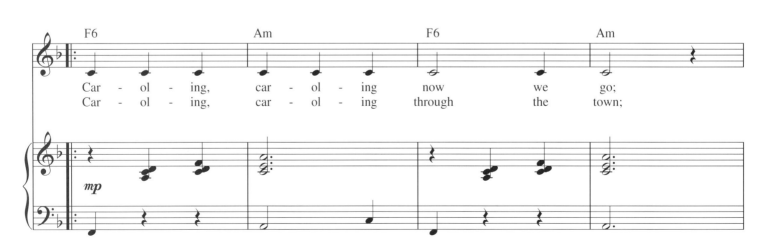

Car - ol - ing, car - ol - ing now we go;
Car - ol - ing, car - ol - ing through the town;

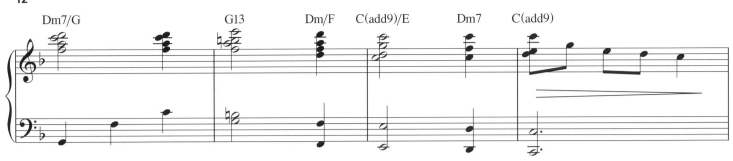

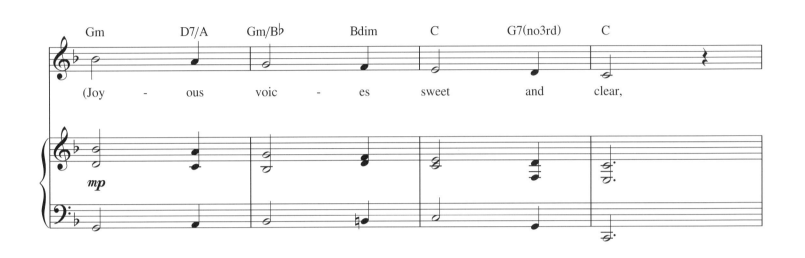

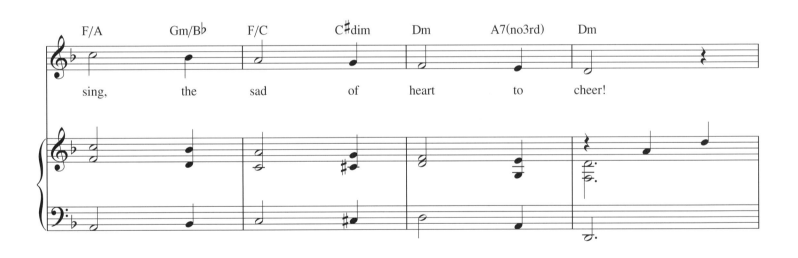

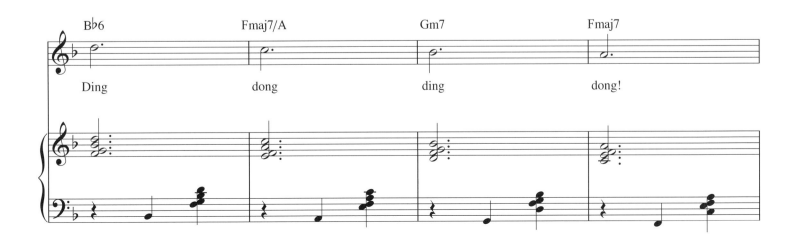

CHRISTMAS IS A-COMIN'
(May God Bless You)

Words and Music by
FRANK LUTHER

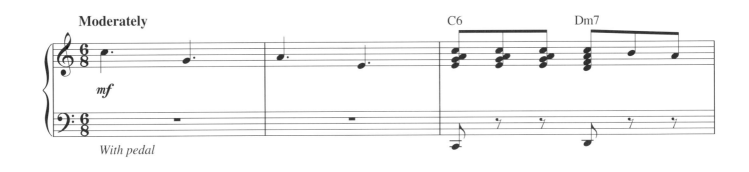

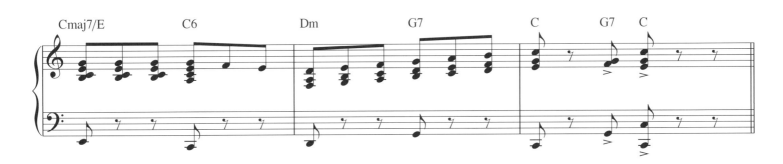

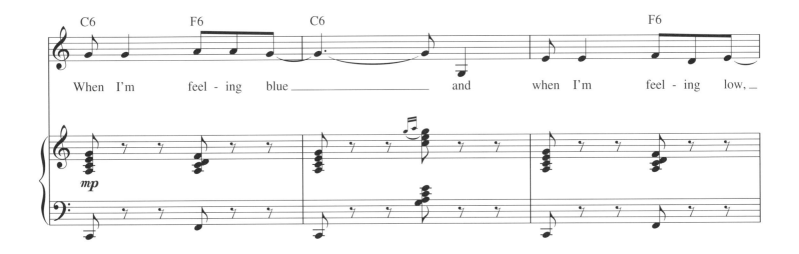

When I'm feel-ing blue _____ and when I'm feel-ing low, __

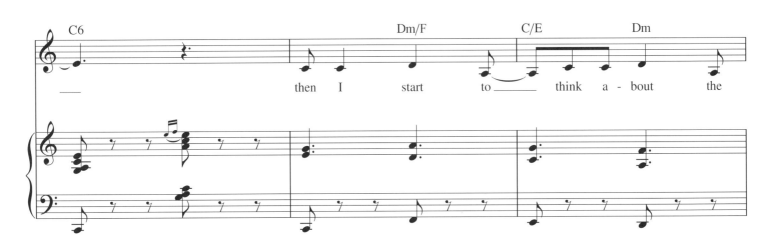

_____ then I start to _____ think a-bout the

friend - ly cat, may God bless you. God bless

you, gen - tle - men, God bless you! If you have - n't got a

friend - ly cat, may God bless you.

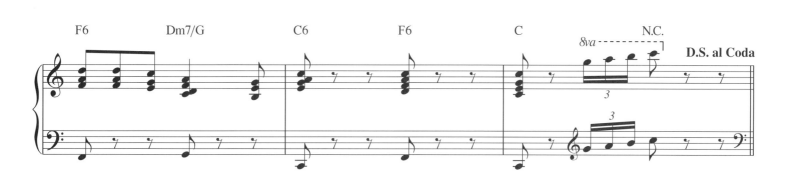

D.S. al Coda

CODA

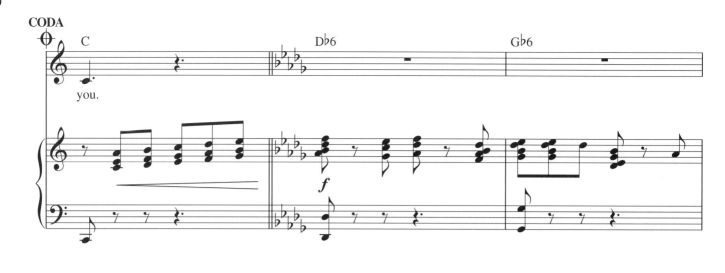

you.

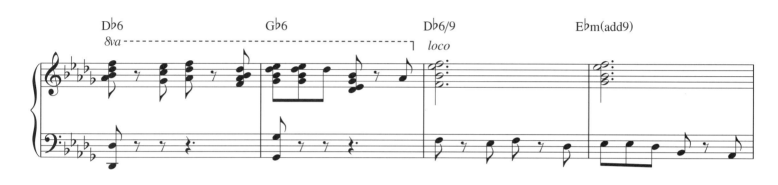

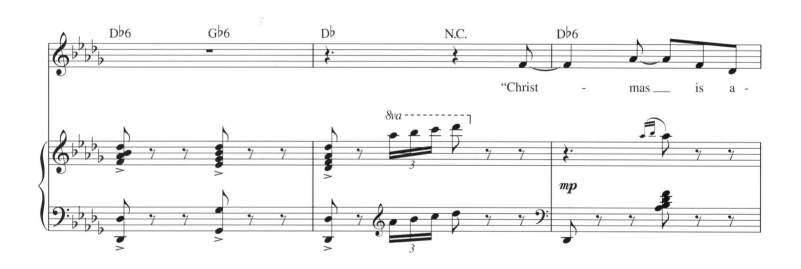

"Christ - mas ___ is a -

com - in', and the ci - der's in the keg. ___ If I

A CHRISTMAS LOVE SONG

Words by ALAN BERGMAN
and MARILYN BERGMAN
Music by JOHNNY MANDEL

Jazz Ballad (straight eighths)

All I want for Christ-mas is you. You're the gift _ that made my dreams _ all come

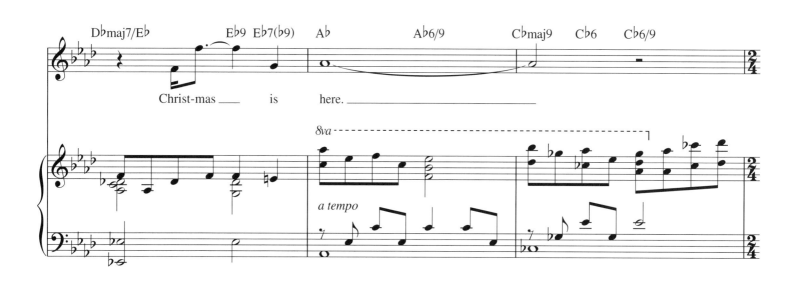

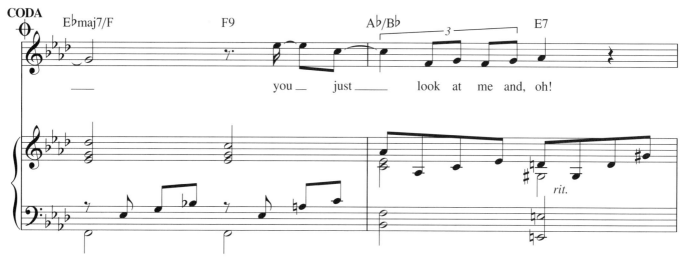

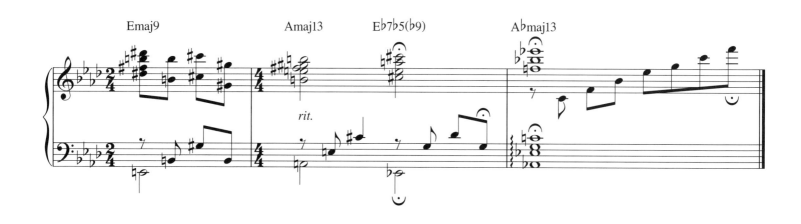

THE CHRISTMAS SONG
(Chestnuts Roasting on an Open Fire)

Music and Lyric by MEL TORME
and ROBERT WELLS

CHRISTMAS TIME IS HERE

from A CHARLIE BROWN CHRISTMAS

Words by LEE MENDELSON
Music by VINCE GUARALDI

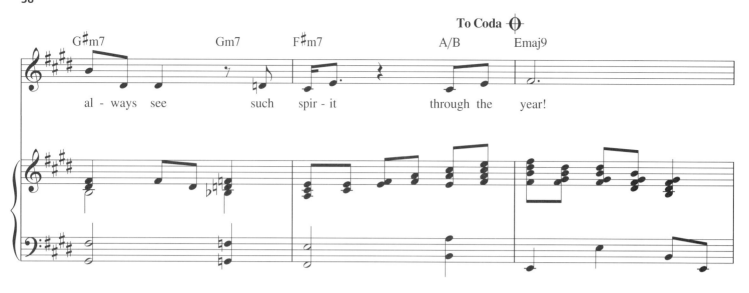

al - ways see such spir - it through the year!

Instrumental solo

Solo ends

THE CHRISTMAS WALTZ

Words by SAMMY CAHN
Music by JULE STYNE

DO YOU HEAR WHAT I HEAR

Words and Music by NOEL REGNEY
and GLORIA SHAYNE

(Do you hear what I hear?) _____

Said the night wind to the lit - tle lamb,
lit - tle lamb to the shep - herd boy,
shep - herd boy to the might - y king,

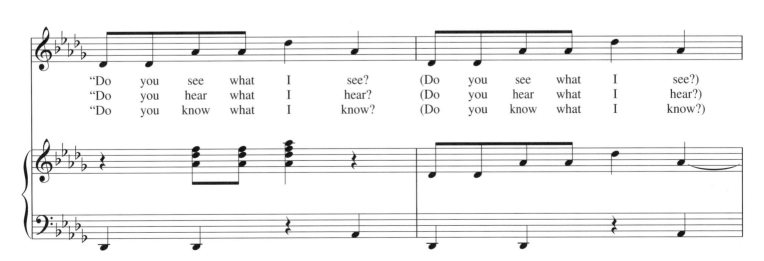

"Do you see what I see? (Do you see what I see?)
"Do you hear what I hear? (Do you hear what I hear?)
"Do you know what I know? (Do you know what I know?)

48

Lis - ten to what I say! _____ The child, the child sleep-ing in the night, He will bring us good - ness and light; He will bring us good - ness and light!" _____

GROWN-UP CHRISTMAS LIST

Words and Music by DAVID FOSTER
and LINDA THOMPSON-JENNER

Slowly, steadily

Faster, very expressively

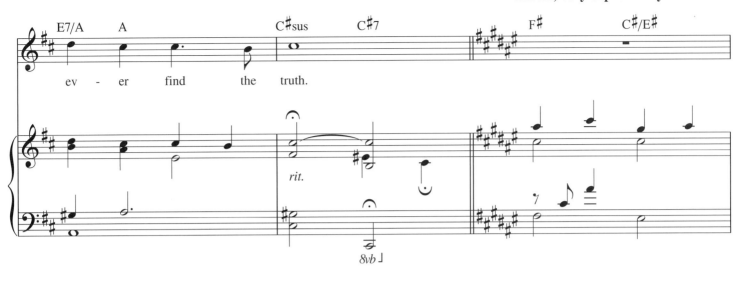

ev - er find the truth.

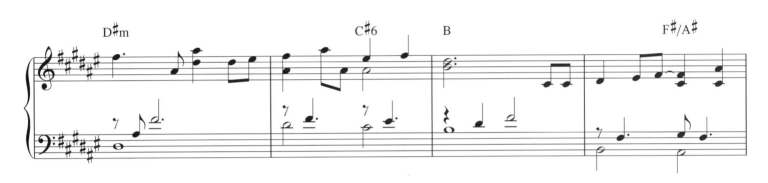

Slowly, steadily

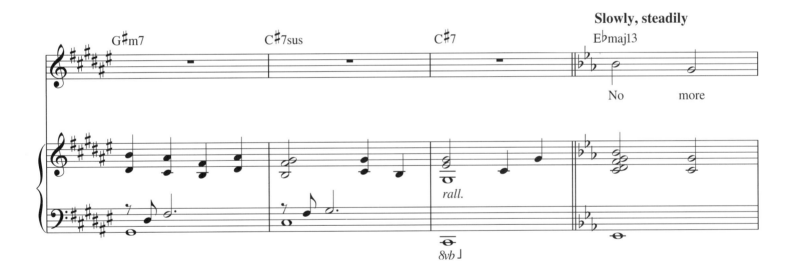

No   more

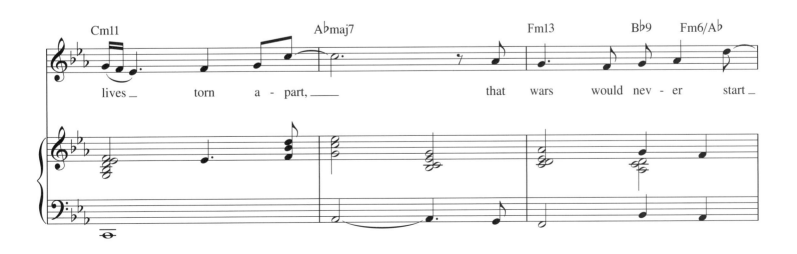

lives _ torn a - part, _____ that wars would nev - er start _

HAPPY XMAS
(War Is Over)

Words and Music by JOHN LENNON
and YOKO ONO

So, this is ___ Christ - mas;

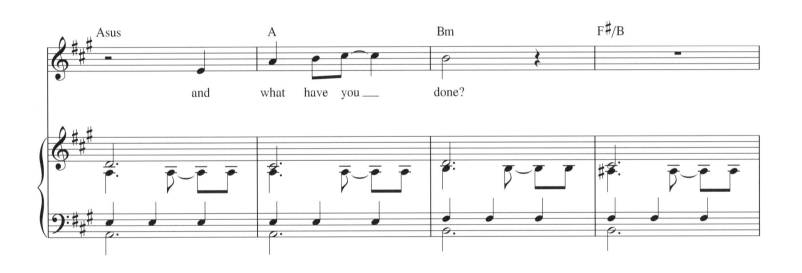

and what have you ___ done?

An - oth - er year o - ver,

HERE COMES SANTA CLAUS
(Right Down Santa Claus Lane)

Words and Music by GENE AUTRY
and OAKLEY HALDEMAN

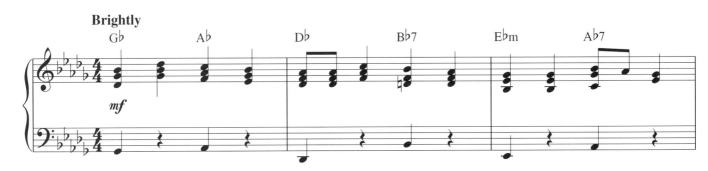

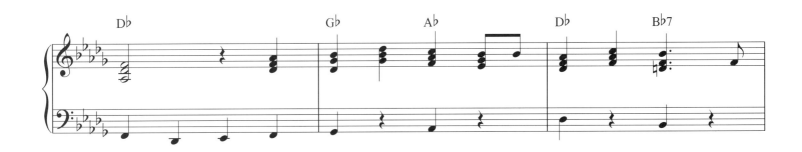

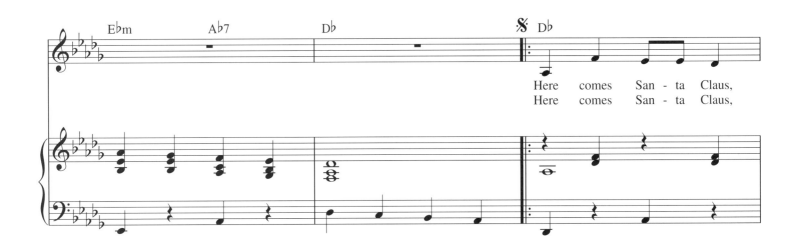

Here comes San-ta Claus,
Here comes San-ta Claus,

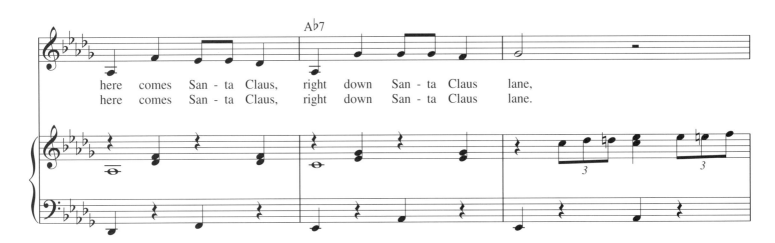

here comes San-ta Claus, right down San-ta Claus lane,
here comes San-ta Claus, right down San-ta Claus lane.

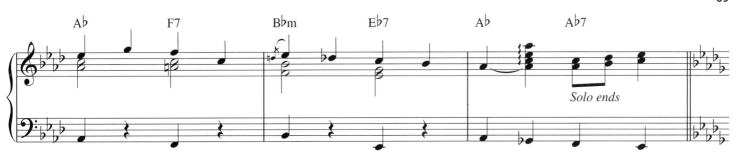

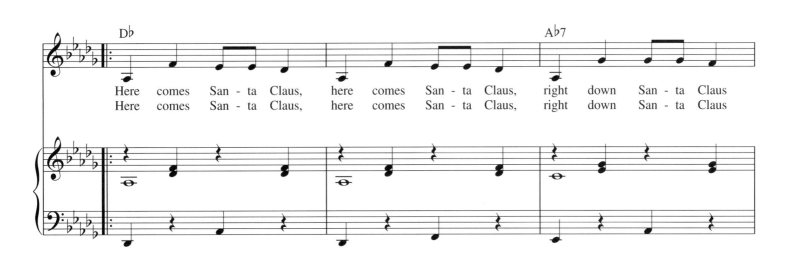

Here comes San - ta Claus, here comes San - ta Claus, right down San - ta Claus
Here comes San - ta Claus, here comes San - ta Claus, right down San - ta Claus

lane.   He   does - n't   care   if   you're
lane;   he'll   come   a - round___   when

rich   or   poor,   he   loves___   you   just   the   same. ___
times   ring   out   that   it's   Christ - mas   morn   a - gain. ___

San - ta Claus knows we're all God's chil - dren; that makes ev - 'ry - thing
Peace __ on earth will come to all if we just fol - low the

right. So fill your hearts with Christ - mas cheer, 'cause
light. So let's give thanks to the Lord a - bove, 'cause

San - ta Claus comes to - night.
San - ta Claus comes to - night.

Instrumental solo

A HOLLY JOLLY CHRISTMAS

Music and Lyrics by
JOHNNY MARKS

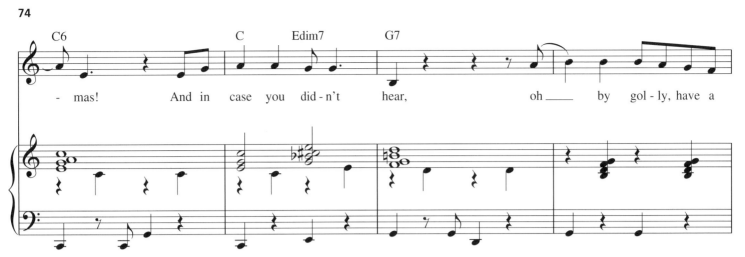

-mas! And in case you did-n't hear, oh ____ by gol-ly, have a

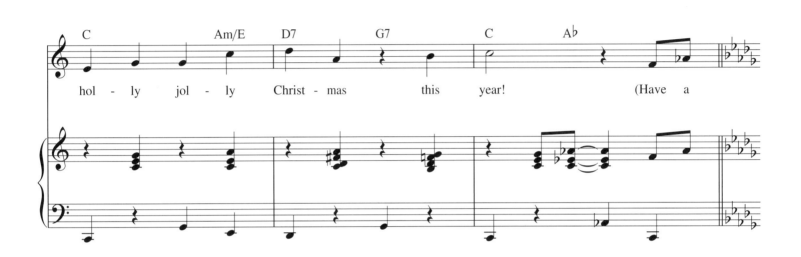

hol - ly jol - ly Christ - mas this year! (Have a

hol - ly jol - ly Christ - mas! It's the best time of the year.) ____ *Instrumental solo*

(There's No Place Like)
HOME FOR THE HOLIDAYS

Words by AL STILLMAN
Music by ROBERT ALLEN

Oh, there's no place like home for the hol-i-days; 'cause no mat-ter how far a-way you roam,

I'LL BE HOME FOR CHRISTMAS

Words and Music by KIM GANNON
and WALTER KENT

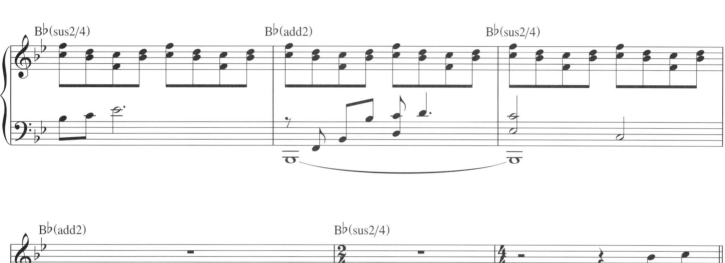

IT'S BEGINNING TO LOOK LIKE CHRISTMAS

By MEREDITH WILLSON

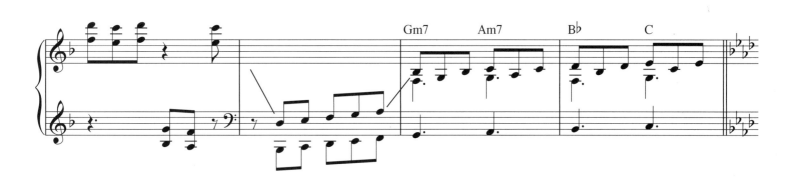

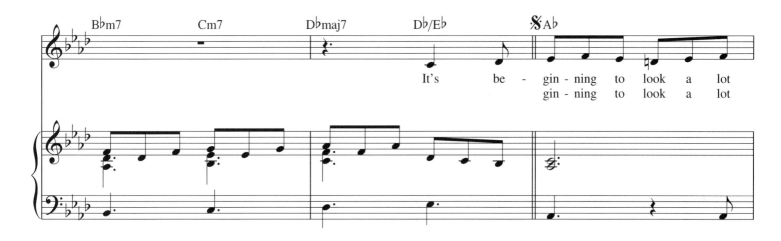

It's be - gin - ning to look a lot
gin - ning to look a lot

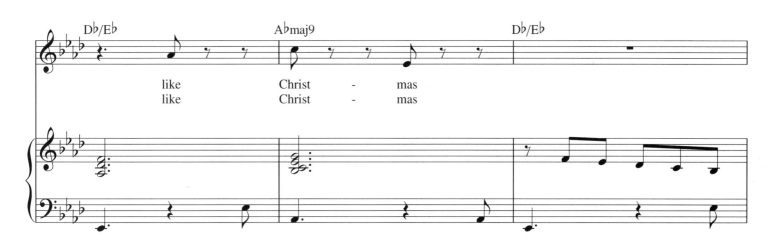

like Christ - mas
like Christ - mas

90

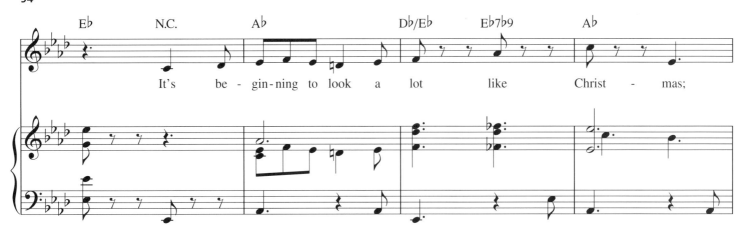

It's be - gin-ning to look a lot like Christ - mas;

soon _____ the bells will start.

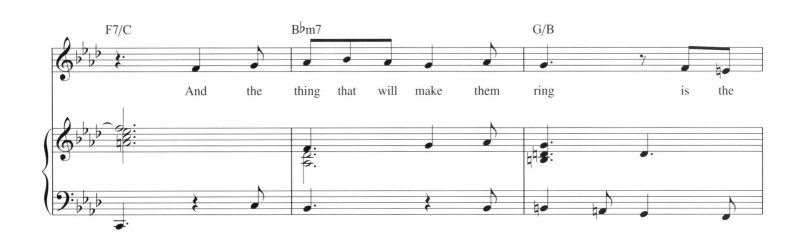

And the thing that will make them ring is the

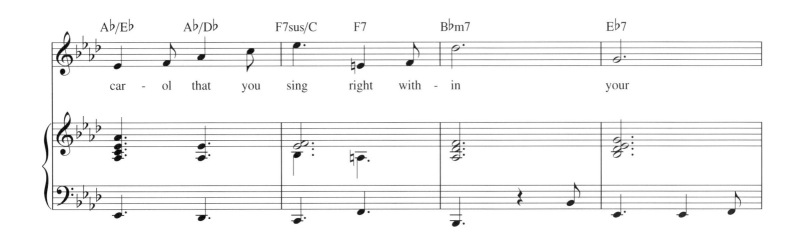

car - ol that you sing right with - in your

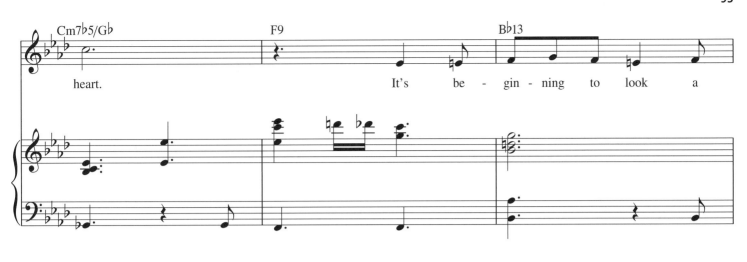

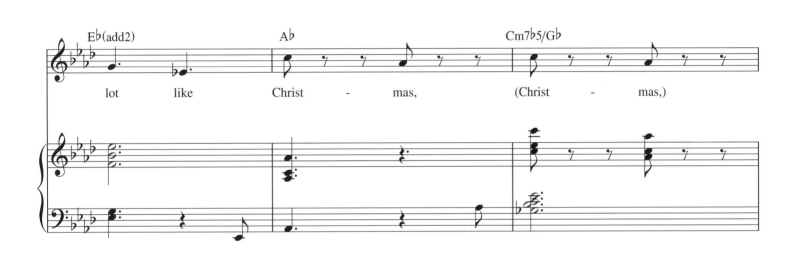

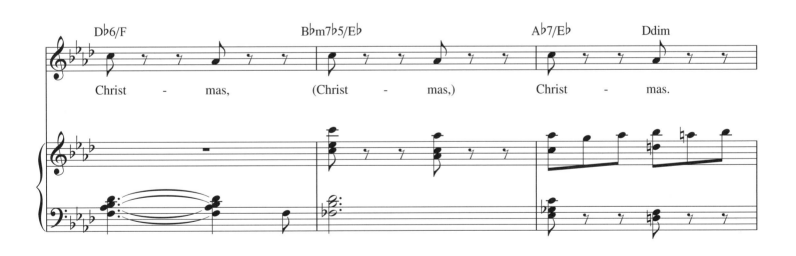

LET IT SNOW! LET IT SNOW! LET IT SNOW!

Words by SAMMY CAHN
Music by JULE STYNE

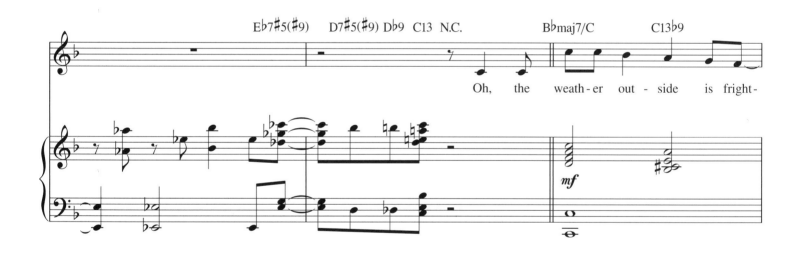

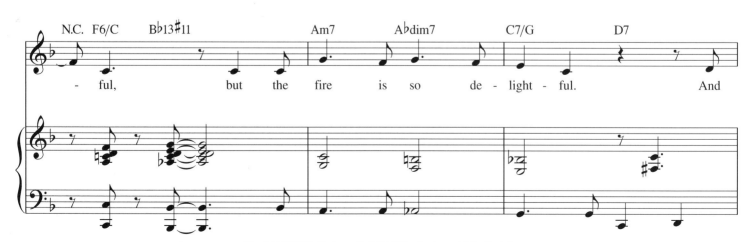

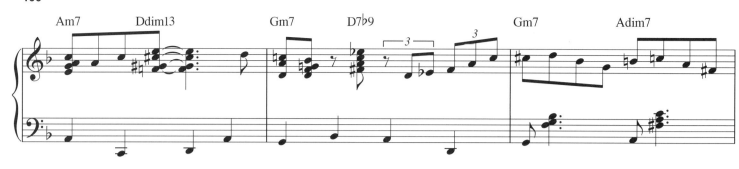

D.S. al Coda

When we

snow! Let it snow! Let it _____ snow!

A MARSHMALLOW WORLD

Words by CARL SIGMAN
Music by PETER DE ROSE

MISTLETOE AND HOLLY

Words and Music by FRANK SINATRA,
DOK STANFORD and HENRY W. SANICOLA

THE MOST WONDERFUL
TIME OF THE YEAR

Words and Music by EDDIE POLA
and GEORGE WYLE

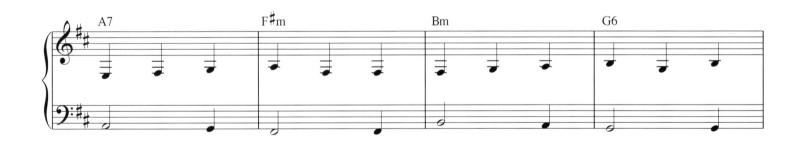

MY FAVORITE THINGS

from THE SOUND OF MUSIC

Lyrics by OSCAR HAMMERSTEIN II
Music by RICHARD RODGERS

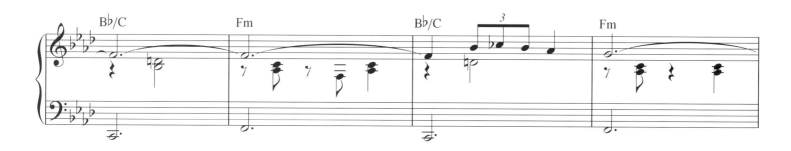

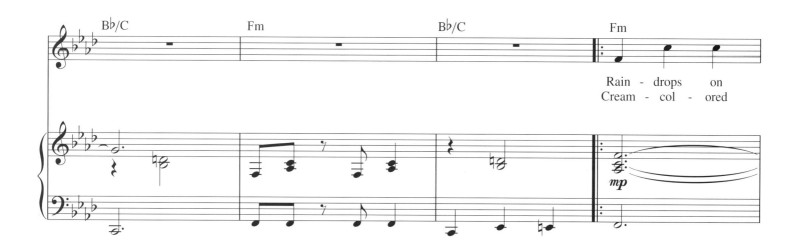

Rain - drops on
Cream - col - ored

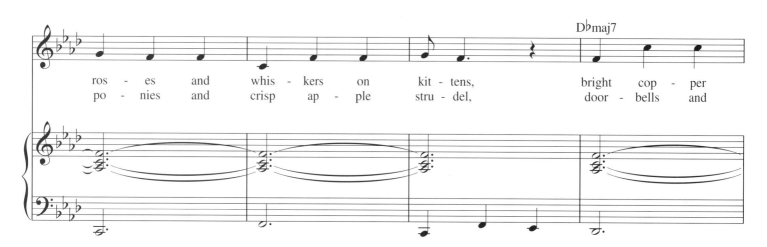

ros - es and whis - kers on kit - tens, bright cop - per
po - nies and crisp ap - ple stru - del, door - bells and

then I don't feel _____ so _____

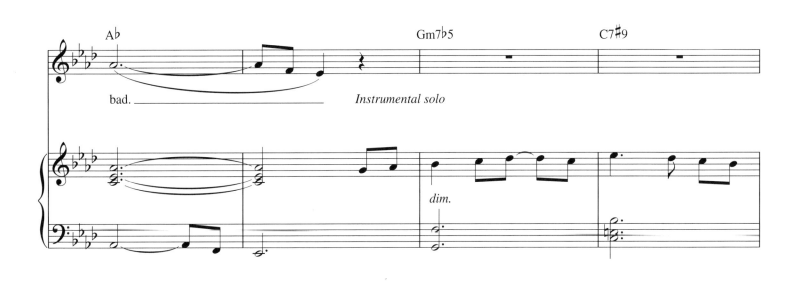

bad. _____ *Instrumental solo*

Girls in white dress - es with

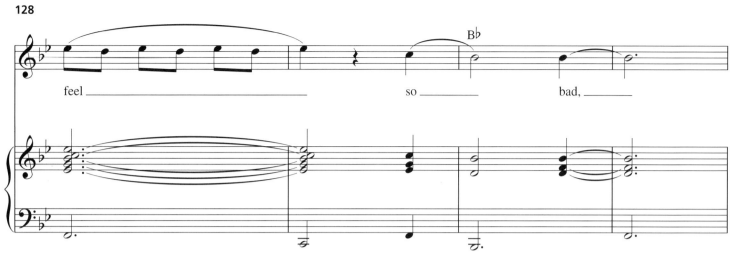

feel _____ so _____ bad, _____

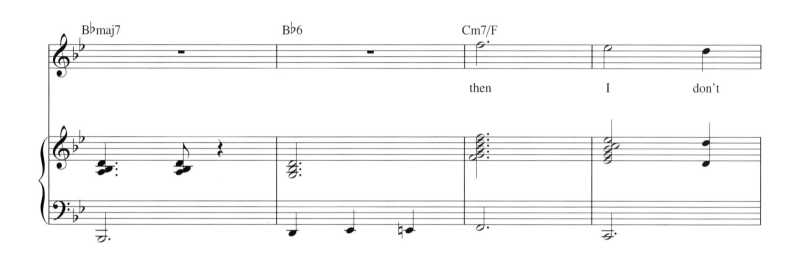

B♭maj7   B♭6   Cm7/F

then   I   don't

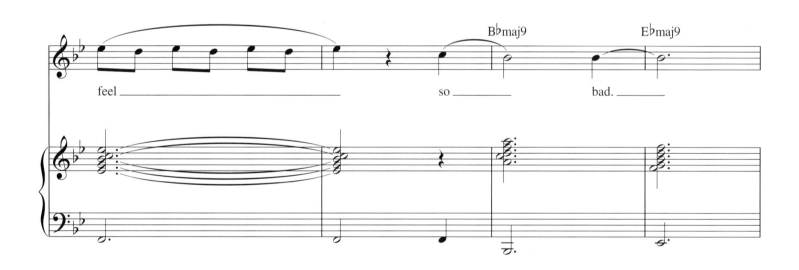

feel _____ so _____ bad. _____

B♭maj9   E♭maj9

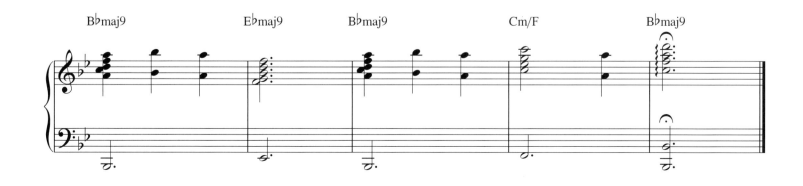

B♭maj9   E♭maj9   B♭maj9   Cm/F   B♭maj9

ROCKIN' AROUND THE CHRISTMAS TREE

Music and Lyrics by
JOHNNY MARKS

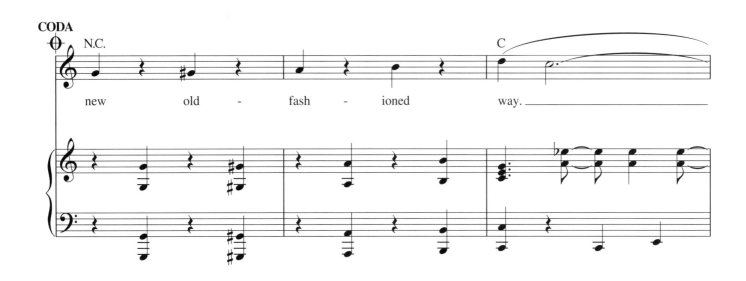

RUDOLPH THE RED-NOSED REINDEER

Music and Lyrics by
JOHNNY MARKS

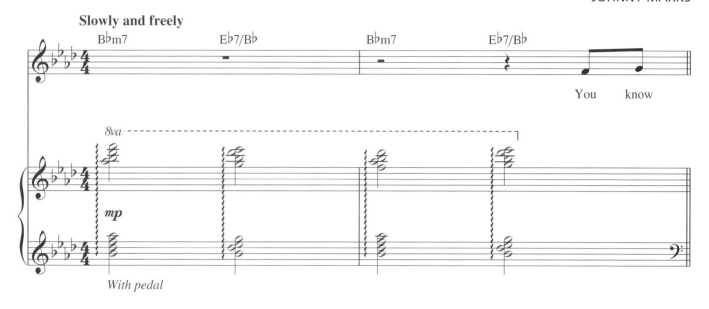

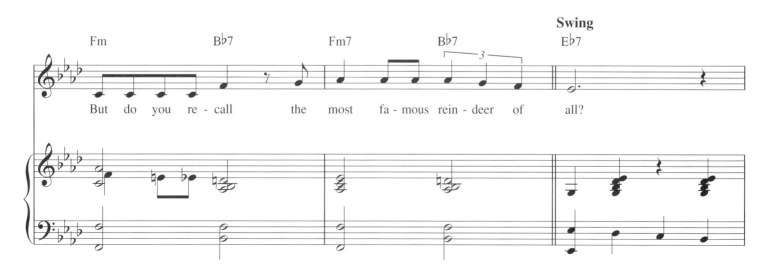

SANTA CLAUS IS COMIN' TO TOWN

Words by HAVEN GILLESPIE
Music by J. FRED COOTS

(You bet-ter watch out!

You bet-ter not cry!

Here's the man who's gon-na tell you why.)

bad or good, ___ so be good, for ___ good - ness sake! ___
toy - land town ___ all a - round the ___ Christ - mas tree. ___

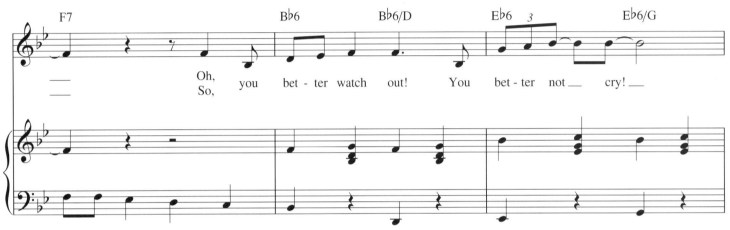

Oh, you bet - ter watch out! You bet - ter not __ cry! __
So, you bet - ter watch out! You bet - ter not __ cry! __

To Coda

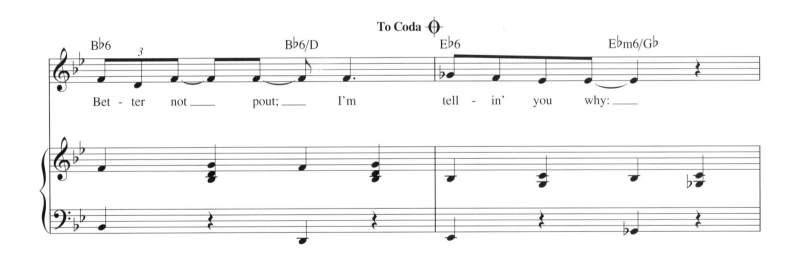

Bet - ter not __ pout; __ I'm tell - in' you why: __

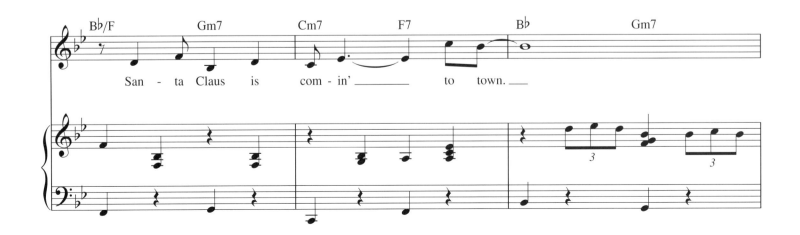

San - ta Claus is com - in' _____ to town. ___

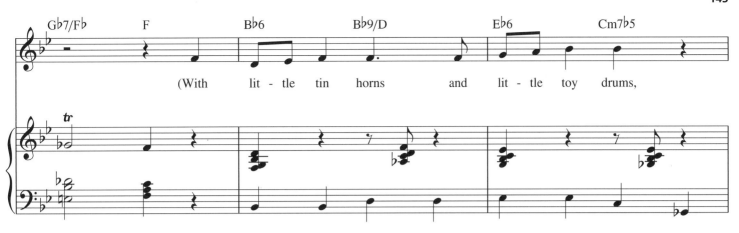

(With lit - tle tin horns and lit - tle toy drums,

root - y toot toots and rum - my tum tums, San - ta Claus is

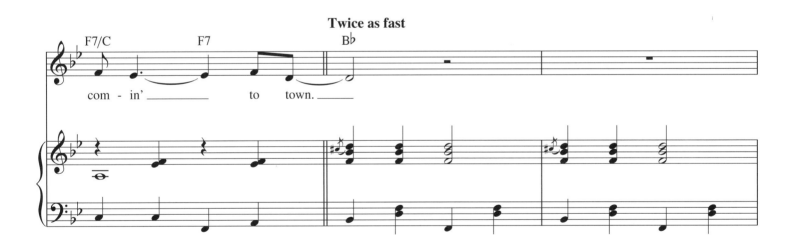

Twice as fast

com - in' _____ to town. _____

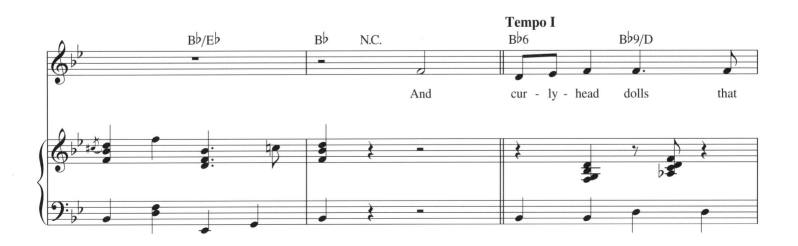

Tempo I

And cur - ly - head dolls that

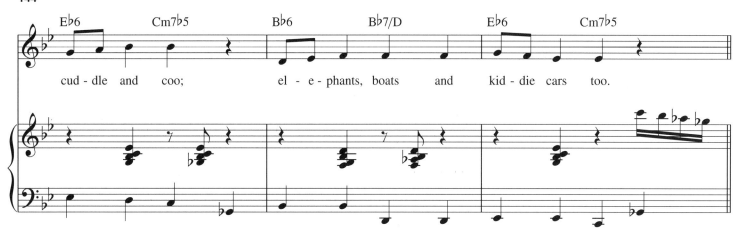

cud - dle and coo; el - e - phants, boats and kid - die cars too.

Twice as fast

San - ta Claus, San - ta Claus, San - ta Claus is

Tempo I   **D.S. al Coda**

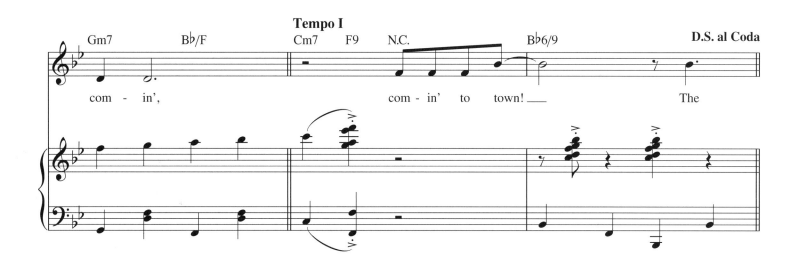

com - in', com - in' to town! ___ The

CODA

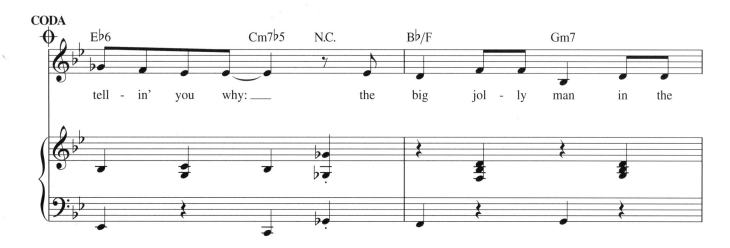

tell - in' you why: ___ the big jol - ly man in the

SILVER BELLS

from the Paramount Picture THE LEMON DROP KID

Words and Music by JAY LIVINGSTON
and RAY EVANS

THIS CHRISTMAS

Words and Music by DONNY HATHAWAY
and NADINE McKINNOR

Hang all the mis-tle-toe; __ I'm gon-na get to know you
Pres - ents and cards I hear; __ my world is filled with cheer and

bet - ter __ this Christ - mas.
you __ this Christ - mas.

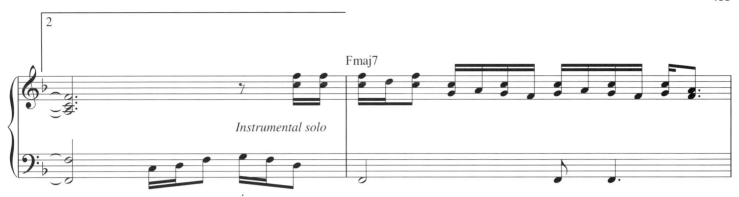

Instrumental solo

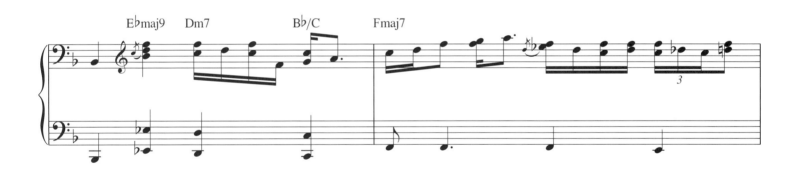

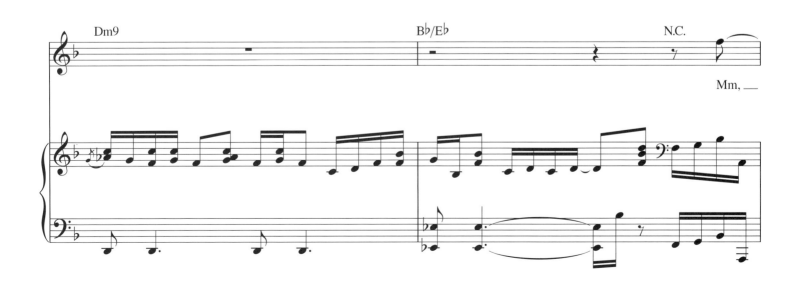

Mm, __

WHITE CHRISTMAS

from the Motion Picture Irving Berlin's HOLIDAY INN

Words and Music by
IRVING BERLIN

ORIGINAL KEYS FOR SINGERS

ACROSS THE UNIVERSE
Because • Blackbird • Hey Jude • Let It Be • Revolution •
Something • and more.
00307010 Vocal Transcriptions with Piano $19.95

LOUIS ARMSTRONG
Dream a Little Dream of Me • Hello, Dolly! • Mack the Knife
• Makin' Whoopee! • Mame • St. Louis Blues • What a
Wonderful World • Zip-A-Dee-Doo-Dah • and more.
00307029 Vocal Transcriptions with Piano $19.99

MARIAH CAREY
Always Be My Baby • Dreamlover • Emotions •
Heartbreaker • Hero • I Don't Wanna Cry • Love Takes
Time • Loverboy • One Sweet Day • Vision of Love • We
Belong Together • and more.
00306835 Vocal Transcriptions with Piano $19.95

PATSY CLINE
Always • Blue Moon of Kentucky • Crazy • Faded Love
• I Fall to Pieces • Just a Closer Walk with Thee • Sweet
Dreams • more. Also includes a biography.
00740072 Vocal Transcriptions with Piano $15.99

ELLA FITZGERALD
A-tisket, A-tasket • But Not for Me • Easy to Love •
Embraceable You • The Lady Is a Tramp • Misty • Oh,
Lady Be Good! • Satin Doll • Stompin' at the Savoy •
Take the "A" Train • and more. Includes a biography and
discography.
00740252 Vocal Transcriptions with Piano $16.95

JOSH GROBAN
Alejate • Awake • Believe • February Song • In Her Eyes •
Now or Never • O Holy Night • Per Te • The Prayer • To
Where You Are • Un Amore Per Sempre • Un Dia Llegara •
You Are Loved (Don't Give Up) • You Raise Me Up • You're
Still You • and more.
00306969 Vocal Transcriptions with Piano $19.99

GREAT FEMALE SINGERS
Cry Me a River (Ella Fitzgerald) • Crazy (Patsy Cline) •
Fever (Peggy Lee) • How Deep Is the Ocean (How High Is
the Sky) (Billie Holiday) • Little Girl Blue (Nina Simone) •
Tenderly (Rosemary Clooney) • and more.
00307132 Vocal Transcriptions with Piano $19.99

GREAT MALE SINGERS
Can't Help Falling in Love (Elvis Presley) • Georgia on My
Mind (Ray Charles) • I've Got the World on a String (Frank
Sinatra) • Mona Lisa (Nat King Cole) • Ol' Man River (Paul
Robeson) • What a Wonderful World (Louis Armstrong)
• and more.
00307133 Vocal Transcriptions with Piano $19.99

BILLIE HOLIDAY
TRANSCRIBED FROM HISTORIC RECORDINGS
Billie's Blues (I Love My Man) • Body and Soul • Crazy He
Calls Me • Easy Living • A Fine Romance • God Bless' the
Child • Lover, Come Back to Me • Miss Brown to You •
Strange Fruit • The Very Thought of You • and more.
00740140 Vocal Transcriptions with Piano $16.95

NANCY LAMOTT
Autumn Leaves • Downtown • I Have Dreamed • It Might
as Well Be Spring • Moon River • Skylark • That Old Black
Magic • and more.
00306995 Vocal Transcriptions with Piano $19.99

LEONA LEWIS – SPIRIT
Better in Time • Bleeding Love • The First Time Ever I Saw
Your Face • Here I Am • Homeless • I Will Be • I'm You's
Whatever It Takes • Yesterday • and more.
00307007 Vocal Transcriptions with Piano $17.95

THE BETTE MIDLER SONGBOOK
Boogie Woogie Bugle Boy • Friends • From a Distance
• The Glory of Love • The Rose • Some People's Lives •
Stay with Me • Stuff like That There • Ukulele Lady • The
Wind Beneath My Wings • and more, plus a fantastic bio
and photos.
00307067 Vocal Transcriptions with Piano $19.99

THE BEST OF LIZA MINNELLI
And All That Jazz • Cabaret • Losing My Mind • Maybe This
Time • Me and My Baby • Theme from "New York, New
York" • Ring Them Bells • Sara Lee • Say Liza (Liza with
a Z) • Shine It On • Sing Happy • The Singer • Taking a
Chance on Love.
00306928 Vocal Transcriptions with Piano $19.99

FRANK SINATRA – MORE OF HIS BEST
Almost like Being in Love • Cheek to Cheek • The Days of
Wine and Roses • Fly Me to the Moon • I Could Write a Book
• In the Wee Small Hours of the Morning • It Might as Well
Be Spring • Luck Be a Lady • Old Devil Moon • Somebody
Loves Me • When the World Was Young • and more.
00307081 Vocal Transcriptions with Piano $19.99

THE VERY BEST OF FRANK SINATRA
Come Fly with Me • I've Got You Under My Skin • It Was a
Very Good Year • My Way • Night and Day • Summer Wind
• The Way You Look Tonight • You Make Me Feel So Young
• and more. Includes biography.
00306753 Vocal Transcriptions with Piano $19.95

STEVE TYRELL – BACK TO BACHARACH
Alfie • Always Something There to Remind Me • Close to
You • I Say a Little Prayer • The Look of Love • Raindrops
Keep Fallin' on My Head • This Guy's in Love with You •
Walk on By • and more.
00307024 Vocal Transcriptions with Piano $16.99

THE BEST OF STEVE TYRELL
Ain't Misbehavin' • Fly Me to the Moon (In Other Words) •
Give Me the Simple Life • I Concentrate on You • I've Got
a Crush on You • In the Wee Small Hours of the Morning •
Isn't It Romantic? • A Kiss to Build a Dream On • Stardust
• The Way You Look Tonight • What a Little Moonlight Can
Do • You'd Be So Nice to Come Home To • and more.
00307027 Vocal Transcriptions with Piano $16.99

SARAH VAUGHAN
Black Coffee • If You Could See Me Now • It Might as
Well Be Spring • My Funny Valentine • The Nearness of
You • A Night in Tunisia • Perdido • September Song •
Tenderly • and more.
00306558 Vocal Transcriptions with Piano $17.95

ANDY WILLIAMS – CHRISTMAS COLLECTION
Blue Christmas • The Christmas Song (Chestnuts Roasting
on an Open Fire) • Do You Hear What I Hear • Happy
Holiday • Kay Thompson's Jingle Bells • The Little
Drummer Boy • The Most Wonderful Time of the Year • O
Holy Night • Sleigh Ride • What Are You Doing New Year's
Eve? • and more. Includes a great bio!
00307158 Vocal Transcriptions with Piano $17.99

ANDY WILLIAMS
Can't Get Used to Losing You • The Days of Wine and Roses
• The Hawaiian Wedding Song (Ke Kali Nei Au) • The Impossible
Dream • Moon River • More • The Most Wonderful Time of
the Year • Red Roses for a Blue Lady • Speak Softly, Love • A
Time for Us • Where Do I Begin • and more.
00307160 Vocal Transcriptions with Piano $17.99

0411

SING WITH THE CHOIR

1. ANDREW LLOYD WEBBER
Any Dream Will Do • As If We Never Said Goodbye • Don't Cry for Me Argentina • Love Changes Everything • Memory • The Music of the Night • Pie Jesu • Whistle down the Wind.
00333001 Book/CD Pack $14.95

2. BROADWAY
Bring Him Home • Cabaret • For Good • Luck Be a Lady • Seasons of Love • There's No Business like Show Business • Where Is Love? • You'll Never Walk Alone.
00333002 Book/CD Pack $14.95

3. STANDARDS
Cheek to Cheek • Georgia on My Mind • I Left My Heart in San Francisco • I'm Beginning to See the Light • Moon River • On the Sunny Side of the Street • Skylark • When I Fall in Love.
00333003 Book/CD Pack $14.95

4. THE 1950s
At the Hop • The Great Pretender • Kansas City • La Bamba • Love Me Tender • My Prayer • Rock Around the Clock • Unchained Melody.
00333004 Book/CD Pack $14.95

5. THE 1960s
All You Need is Love • Can't Help Falling in Love • Dancing in the Street • Good Vibrations • I Heard It Through the Grapevine • I'm a Believer • Under the Boardwalk • What a Wonderful World.
00333005 Book/CD Pack $14.95

6. THE 1970s
Ain't No Mountain High Enough • Bohemian Rhapsody • I'll Be There • Imagine • Let It Be • Night Fever • Yesterday Once More • You Are the Sunshine of My Life.
00333006 Book/CD Pack $14.95

7. DISNEY FAVORITES
The Bare Necessities • Be Our Guest • Circle of Life • Cruella De Vil • Friend like Me • Hakuna Matata • Joyful, Joyful • Under the Sea.
00333007 Book/CD Pack $14.95

8. DISNEY HITS
Beauty and the Beast • Breaking Free • Can You Feel the Love Tonight • Candle on the Water • Colors of the Wind • A Whole New World (Aladdin's Theme) • You'll Be in My Heart • You've Got a Friend in Me.
00333008 Book/CD Pack $14.95

9. LES MISÉRABLES
At the End of the Day • Bring Him Home • Castle on a Cloud • Do You Hear the People Sing? • Finale • I Dreamed a Dream • On My Own • One Day More.
00333009 Book/CD Pack $14.99

10. CHRISTMAS FAVORITES
Frosty the Snow Man • The Holiday Season • (There's No Place Like) Home for the Holidays • Little Saint Nick • Merry Christmas, Darling • Santa Claus Is Comin' to Town • Silver Bells • White Christmas.
00333011 Book/CD Pack $14.95

11. CHRISTMAS TIME IS HERE
Blue Christmas • Christmas Time is Here • Feliz Navidad • Happy Xmas (War Is Over) • I'll Be Home for Christmas • Let It Snow! Let It Snow! Let It Snow! • We Need a Little Christmas • Wonderful Christmastime.
00333012 Book/CD Pack $14.95

12. THE SOUND OF MUSIC
Climb Ev'ry Mountain • Do-Re-Mi • Edelweiss • The Lonely Goatherd • My Favorite Things • So Long, Farewell • The Sound of Music.
00333019 Book/CD Pack $14.99

13. CHRISTMAS CAROLS
Angels We Have Heard on High • Deck the Hall • Go, Tell It on the Mountain • Joy to the World • O Come, All Ye Faithful (Adeste Fideles) • O Holy Night • Silent Night • We Wish You a Merry Christmas.
00333020 Book/CD Pack $14.99

14. GLEE
Can't Fight This Feeling • Don't Stop Believin' • Jump • Keep Holding On • Lean on Me • No Air • Rehab • Somebody to Love.
00333059 Book/CD Pack $16.99

15. HYMNS
Abide with Me • All Hail the Power of Jesus' Name • Amazing Grace • Be Still My Soul • Blessed Assurance • The Church's One Foundation • Come, Thou Almighty King • It Is Well with My Soul.
00333158 Book/CD Pack $14.99

16. WORSHIP
All Hail the Power of Jesus' Name • And Can It Be That I Should Gain • Everlasting God • Glory to God Forever • Here I Am to Worship • How Great Is Our God • I Will Rise • A Mighty Fortress Is Our God • My Jesus, I Love Thee • Shout to the Lord • You Are My King (Amazing Love) • Your Name.
00333170 Book/CD Pack $14.99

FOR MORE INFORMATION, SEE YOUR LOCAL MUSIC DEALER,
OR WRITE TO:

HAL•LEONARD®
CORPORATION
7777 W. BLUEMOUND RD. P.O. BOX 13819 MILWAUKEE, WI 53213

Prices, contents, and availability
subject to change without notice.

0511